DIY Wood Pallet Projects

Over 35 Design Ideas For Beginner

ALEXANDER ADELHARD

COPYRIGHT ©

TABLE OF C(

INTRODUCTION

Trying to figure out what a pallet is? Here is a simple definition. A pallet is a flat structure for the shipment of cargo. It gives support to goods while being lifted by a forklift, front loader or a pallet jack. They are usually made of pieces of wood and vary in size. Some of them are made up of fiber and plastic.

Most of the pallets are made of wood and the containers are secured with straps or shrink wrap, for the purpose of shipping. Pallets were invented in the twentieth century and their continued use has lead to different designs and forms. They work well with modern packaging, commonly used for shipping.

They have been used for a long time. Designers have introduced a variety into the market, thereby giving more options and choice of freedom. A transporter will just have to make the right choice that suits their needs.

Wooden pallets are commonly used because they are environment-friendly, cheap and long lasting. They can also be easily reused since they can be modified to various shapes, unlike the plastic pallets that cannot be easily deformed to desired shapes. Generally, they form part of the transport equipment. A typical wooden pallet looks like this.

CHAPTER ONE

WHAT YOU NEED TO KNOW ABOUT WOODEN PALLETS

As mentioned, wooden pallets are structures that form a base for the utilization of goods in the process of the supply chain. They can also be used for storage and stacking purposes, as well as transportation. It is the most common base for a unit load, inclusive of the load and pallet. One thing about the pallets is that most of them become useless for transportation when the goods reach their destination. A creative mind will make use of them thereafter.

They are designed to give support to heavy loads; this offers a guarantee that they are capable of making other objects, for use at home and for commercial purposes. They are durable, meaning that they can last longer. Pallets are made from pieces of timber, combined together to form a structure that is strong enough to hold loads. Their durability is trustworthy, because they are from natural timber and they have to meet the standards of the manufacturing process.

Wooden pallets are long-lasting, compared to plastic pallets. In essence, wooden pallets can stay useful for a period of 8 to 10 years; most people create furniture to be used at home and offices. Before wooden pallets are manufactured or assembled, they must be proven to be strong enough and have the ability to last longer than the transportation period. Some people have discovered that they are better than the normal timber that is used in the assembly of furniture.

They are also much cheaper compared to normal timber. Products made from pallets are usually cheap and readily available. The method by which wooden pallets are made makes them reliable, since they are treated, and this can be a good material for the assembly of furniture that is to be used for years and for a special reason.

The chemicals used are part of wood treatment, compared to timber that is used from its natural set up. For so many years, wood has been treated with heat and chemicals for their longevity to make more reliable wood pallets. Wooden pallets are appealing to the eye, especially when they are being used for handling goods during transportation.

One more thing about the wooden pallet is that they are environment-friendly; they are biodegradable and don't have a negative impact on the environment; in essence, destroying them by fire it does not emit dangerous carbon smoke to the atmosphere. Wooden pallets are not always burnt because they are still useful; burning isn’t the best idea, unless they are no longer useful. They are also resistant to high temperatures in relation to plastic pallets.

There is a notion that plastic pallets are taking over the wooden pallets; this is incorrect because plastics are hazardous to the environment and cannot be easily reused. By the time plastic pallets are used, they become deformed rendering them not reusable.

Wooden pallets will reduce the rate at which forests are being depleted in search of timber and can provide another source for the supply of timber as an alternative to small units. Wooden pallets are economical friendly, given the fact that timber products are expensive nowadays. Products made of pallets are cheaper and guarantee safety.

The heat treatment of the wooden pallets not only reduces the moisture content but also changes the natural composition of the wood, making it resistant to the absorption of moisture in the near future. The treatment also makes the wood to have a reasonable weight, which is an added advantage for its reuse at home for furniture. On the other hand, the lighter weight reduces its cost and will provide safety for your goods, since it won't be attacked by microorganisms, such as fungi and mold.

Having mentioned the treatment, it implies that most of the heat-treated timber does not contain chemicals that can be dangerous for humans, though it is advisable to add furnish to get rid of the natural smell that comes with timber. The difference between the wooden pallet and natural timber is the cost, where the wooden pallet can be cheap because it is second-hand and comes in different or cut sizes. In the recent years, they have been designed to have wheels to enable easy mobility. If a wooden pallet with wheels was to be designed to a bed, how would it be having a bed with wheels? I believe this would be an invention of itself.

MINOR FACTS ABOUT WOODEN PALLETS

- Wooden pallets come in various categories and designs, but the major classifications are the stringer pallets and the block pallets. The stringer contains frames that are parallel to each other. The frames are called the stringer. The deck boards are fixed to the frames and that makes a pallet.
- An ordinary sized pallet has three frames, which helps in making it firm and gives the ability to be used for heavier loads. Some of the stringer pallets contain a notch so they can be picked up from any four directions. This means that they have a four-way entry.
- The block pallets are much stronger than the stringer pallets because they utilize the parallel stringers as well as the perpendicular stringers for efficient handling of loads. It is also known as the four-way pallet because a pallet jack can be used from any side when moving it.
- All of the above-mentioned types of pallets are mostly made up of softwood, making it easier to dismantle and reuse for other purposes.
- Other types of pallets include the eco pellets that are made of paper that are good for lighter loads and can be easily rebranded, compared to plastic pallets.
- Another major, however expensive pallet, is the aluminum pallet. It is lighter than steel and plastic pallets. They are expensive because they are the most effective and mostly used for air freight, military transport and sea storage.

- Steel pallets are strong and used for heavier loads, high stacking loads and long-term dry storage. The excellent pallets are made up of carbon steel. Discarded wooden pallets must not be used as firewood; they can be utilized for pallet crafts and reasonable pieces of furniture.
- Considering the fact that wood is used in almost all industries, it is important to give it the importance that it deserves. When it comes to the utilization of used wooden pallets, it should be understood that they are basically timber but made for specific work.
- There is no difference between the timber that you buy from a yard and that which is meant for the pallets. For your information, timber meant for the construction of pallets is of high quality such that if used for other purposes it will give you the best results.
- Wood pallets are used to transport goods all over the world; can you try and imagine how many tons of timber will be enough for the work? It cannot be

an easy task to come up with the right figures because it is not confined to one place.

- In other words, we are trying to see how the discarded wooden pallet can be reused for other things. It is clear that it is used for load support, but can it give you other products? When we say wooden pallets that have been discarded, it does not mean that it's useless. This implies that the wooden pallet is weak for its job but strong enough to make other products.
- When a wooden pallet is termed as discarded, it means that it has finished its work of transportation, and then it can be returned to the owners. Or, if the cost of transportation was inclusive of the pallet, then it belongs to the owner of the goods or loads on transit.

Easy to Plan And Start Doing It Yourself

There are a number of wooden pallets that have been left for no use; people have started using them for making furniture and other important activities. The reason for the use of wooden pallets in the pallet craft industry is that pallets are readily available and cheap, compared to normal timber that can be bought from the yards and sawmills. It is also important to note that most of the regulations of handling timber have been made difficult by the governments, due to deforestation.

This is to encourage people to make use of the materials available so that the trees can be preserved. When we resort to the wooden pallets as an alternative source of wood, we will make our forests preserved for the future generations and also the climate will be friendly.

If the wood has been considered as the best material for the construction of pallets, it means that without wood, the various economic sectors cannot move on or will soon stop operating. It should be encouraged by the concerned authorities that the natural resource of wood should be used carefully.

These can be done by making sure that the used pieces of pallet wood must be considered as an alternative to timber. Discarded wooden pallets can be reused for several purposes, if you are not informed.

They can replace the expensive timber, from the forests, to make furniture, and other equipment like the garden tools and machinery. Long before metals were invented, timber was used as vehicle chases. We have seen houses that have been constructed by leftover wooden pallets and have proven to work.

The floor of some houses have been covered by wooden pallets; this has provided an exceptional shelter for society. Wooden pallets can also be used to construct houses for domesticated animals like dogs, goose, turkey, horses and much more. As a beginner, you must believe that wooden pallets cannot only be used for pallets; they have the ability to offer the best for other utilizations.

There are many ideas that you can do by yourself and also provide high-class comfort. One advantage of wooden pallets is that they can be used as it is. One has to make a few adjustments to suit their needs. Cutting it is very simple because it was already prepared and it is easily dismantled. One may come to the conclusion that pallets are very small structures, such that the wood cannot provide the required size to meet the furniture construction, but this idea is void because we have three categories of pallets. The large ones that range between 5 meters and 6 meters, the medium-sized wooden pallet, which is approximately 4 meters, and the small ones that come in different sizes. The variety of sizes demands wood of different sizes to construct them. This provides a large variety of choices to construct a number of furniture and structures, like this sample.

They are easily joined together. Wooden pallet projects do not require advanced skills for one to succeed in; it takes common knowledge to come up with ideas. You are very free to start suspecting that the beds and seats that you use in your office and home are made up of wood from discarded wooden pallets; why should someone struggle to buy expensive wood to construct a cow pen while the wood from discarded wooden pallets can serve the same purpose? Let us see the various categories that this important product can be utilized in our daily life, in the following chapters.

CHAPTER TWO

LIVING ROOM FURNITURE

It is amazing to see a pallet living room. A living room should be decorated to give the required desired look, for it is the room that your visitors will be hosted. We all want a place that will add value to us. When people come to your home, you will be in a good position to start narrating how unique your living room is. It is also a place where you can use to market your pallet craft products. A living room with pallet furniture looks enlightened and expensively decorated. The modern living room should provide a sense of belonging to the owners, providing a platform for new people in their home to rate the owner positively.

In this generation, where global warming and natural resources are getting exhausted, the major objective of every industry is sustainability in construction materials. Wooden pallet leftovers can help in the supply of interior and exterior building materials. What is demanded of a living room is not the expense that comes with the furniture but the comfort and its presentation; it should have a clear class of furniture that has originality and taste. All the characteristics of a modern living room can be introduced by furniture made from wooden pallets.

Pallets do have a great potential, if utilized well. One can make anything out of pallets at a decent price. They can be used without dismantling them or they can be broken into boards and come up with a structure for furniture. When they are broken down, they make perfect building material. Wood from an old wooden pallet is beautiful, which is perfect for creating texture on walls and displayable items.

Pallets do come in different categories, as mentioned. It is important to consider that depending on what you want, this determines the type of pallets that you will acquire. One thing that is common with it is that they are cheap and affordable. Some are free because in some organizations they have occupied space and they consider giving them out for free. It only requires a mental preparedness to start embracing wood pallets, so you succeed in pallet crafting.

QUALITIES OF A GOOD LIVING ROOM

There are several characteristics that would define a good living room, but it does not mean that it should be expensive or equipped with great furniture for it to be considered high quality. There are some other considerations that should be made so a living room becomes excellent. The kind of furniture that is brought into a living room will determine its quality. Before you purchase furniture for a living room, you must take into consideration the cost and the level of comfort that you want.

Another thing that must be factored in is what kind of work is going to be done in the living room. This is important because, in some families, you will find that people use the living room as a study area. In other words, a living room should look eye catching. It must be designed to give the needed relaxed atmosphere. For a living room to have similar quality of a modern one, you ought to make sure that the furniture is unique and sourced from professionals.

WOODEN PALLET CHAIRS

One of the ways of making your living room stand out is by introducing furniture that cannot be found anyhow from the stores. One idea is making use of the wooden pallet to come up with the best and unique living room chair and couches. It goes without doubt that pallet furniture has been the leading source of the furniture of its own.

We should not have the ideology that expensive is the best; we believe that wooden pallets are very cheap but they are known to have been used for the construction of the best couches that has been admired by many. Looking at the furniture that can be found in an average living room, you will realize that they have the same purpose all over; you do not have to worry about anyone asking you the reason why you admire pallet wood furniture. What is important is the fact that it is unique and gives the service that every other furniture can give.

Pallet Living Room Tables

Wooden pallet tables last longer compared to those that have been constructed by normal wood. This is because the pallet wood has gone through a process of preservation and was used for transport. This makes the wood have attractive, visible veins. Furniture made of pallet wood will last for a long time, and they are easily repaired because the size of the pallets are readily available and can are easily cut to fix broken or weak furniture. In essence, when it comes to its repair, pallet wood is uniform and the new wood will fit in the old one, without demanding an expensive finish. Furniture that is mostly found in a modern living room ix prone to water because children love being in the living room. Thanks to the treated pallet wood, it is resistant to wet conditions because the moisture absorption is very low compared to normal timber. Wooden pallets will give your living room a unique appearance that every visitor will be left with many questions.

It is practical to choose furniture that is reasonably priced and you will find that the reasonable price is from the wooden pallets. We know the price of the pallet wood can be an issue, but it is not as expensive compared to other materials. Modern furniture, from pallet wood, can be found in reputable stores and you can also learn about pallet craft, since it is not hard. Pallet wood furniture is also long lasting. The most important thing about pallet wood furniture is they should be constructed well for better practicality and functionality.

Wooden pallet furniture will offer you a variety of sizes that you need. Depending on the size and shape of the furniture that you desire, pallet wood comes in various sizes and are easily converted to usable furniture in the living room. It is important to note it is not mandatory to dismantle the whole pallet into pieces; it can be used as it is. For instance, two pallets joined together top to top can give you a very comfortable bed at a cheap price. What would be the difference when you wake up from a pallet bed and when you wake up from an ordinary bed, the truth be told, there is no difference at all. Pallet furniture will look unique because it can be designed easily into various designs and styles.

Pallet Televisions Set Stands

Pallet furniture is not easily broken, since they are designed to handle all manner of weights in the transportation industry. If we translate this to furniture, that is going to be used in a modern living room, it will give you the best long-term service, compared to the usual timber from a yard. Consider a television stand that is made from pallet wood, it is has a high chance to last longer because the wood is strong and is not strained by the weight of the TV.

Let’s talk briefly about this stand because as we know very well that electronic equipment are very expensive and they need to be handled with care, The normal stand do come with some defects from the shops, pallets will give you an original look as well as the surety of not being broken due to the weight of the TV. The sofas that are made up of the pallet wood are very comfortable and can handle all weights of people that seat on it.

They are also free to move around with because they can easily be dismantled and be moved to other areas of the living room. The couches made from pallet wood will give room to be convertible to a bed which can be an added advantage when you have very many visitors, due to its simplicity. We all leave in houses that belong to us or belong to other people. At some point in life, we will want to change the residential place or renovate the area. During renovation time, most of the furniture in the houses is moved outside and this can be a very challenging activity. Some of the furniture can easily be broken down, more especially those that have permanent joints. Pallet furniture is easily repairable and can be broken into pieces for easier mobility. When one is relocating to a different house, pallet furniture can be dismantled and be fixed easily to the vehicles without much considerations of time. There are very many designs that are on the market and many of them are being formulated every day. As we mentioned, you only need to appreciate the wooden pallets and have the mindset of utilizing the locally available raw materials for home improvement.

Wooden Pallet Bookshelves

Home and office furniture are of various kinds and we are not limited to any one of them, being of one standard design. The book shelve, for example, is one of the home accessories that can be made from pallets and provide long-lasting security to your books. A pallet table is another type of furniture that can be designed from discarded wooden pallets. One benefit is that the table from this material cannot be joined using the normal nails and joints. The can be grooved to form fixable joints and come up with a strong, long-lasting table. There are a number of designs for tables but this depends on the purpose of the table. We can have the tables meant for reading, coffee tables, small, and large tables for different occasions. The tables come in many different shapes, like rectangular, oval, square, circular and triangular. The wooden pallets can easily be converted to shapes in regard to the desired furniture.

PALLET LIVING ROOM DRAWER TABLES

Tables made of pallet wood can be fixed with drawers, as in they are simply compatible with the plan. This is possible because they have two layers in between the stringers, where the space for the drawers can be fixed.

A good number of people have not discovered that pallets can be good materials for a lovely interior design. A good pallet craft will give your living room a classical look, if well designed. Pallet craft has been ignored by many, due to the fact that it uses timber. For someone who understands the cost of wood, in this generation, will always be going for the pallets. For your information, wood is wood but the difference is how is it treated. The treatment of timber from the yard matters when determining the work it is intended to do. Pallet wood is the best because pallet construction is regulated to meet a certain standard. This is the reason as to why it is good for furniture construction.

Arm chairs are another type of furniture that wood pallets have been known for. They are beautiful and provide elegance, if well planned. They can be made to have the best sitting posture and can be adjusted to different sizes. The living room should be a place that can create stories in the way it is designed. It does not mean that pallets can only be used for furniture alone; they can also be used for the walls and the ceiling board. A pallet wall appears original and one of a kind.

A ceiling that is crafted by discarded pallet materials looks very good and it adds security to the home. Most of the ceiling boards that are used don't last for more than 15 years before they are worn off or invaded by termites. The pallet ceiling board will last longer than normal ceiling boards.

In between the roof and the ceiling, this area can be converted to a small storage because the base, which is the pallet wood is firm, and can hold heavy loads. They will give your house assurance that the wood-eating pests cannot come near your house because the pallet wood was already treated. Apart from that, the house will be creatively designed with cheap materials from discarded wooden pallets. It is a fact that the living room is a basic place in every family house; not all of us have the potential to afford the most expensive furniture in the world. However, one can find something financially small and come up with good furniture for their home. The wooden pallet projects are affordable to anyone and free to use creatively.

We all have a different taste and we believe the pallets can help give us the chance to create something we have always desired in life. There are so many ideas, and furniture that can be put in the living room, depending on individualistic needs. Pallet ideas are very dynamic; people come up with them on a daily basis. They cannot be exhausted; if there is something you have always admired, it is time to think about how you can start a pallet craft project. The pallet can be found anywhere transportation is done. You can also buy pallet wood from the suppliers and use them for your construction. A house that is built using pallet wood simply matches with pallet furniture and this gives a perfect blend. Some advice; pallet wood is not easily burnt, because it has been hardened by heat and treated, unlike the other houses that are easily consumed by fire.

CHAPTER THREE

WOODEN PALLET KITCHEN FURNITURE

The kitchen is one of the most frequently used places in the house; it is not exceptional for pallet projects. You can have everything in the kitchen made up of pallet wood. A poorly arranged kitchen can make you lose the passion for making food and you will find the kitchen not conducive for you to cook. You cannot afford to have your kitchen look like a disaster, yet the pallets are all over for you to create a gorgeous kitchen and have a better place to cook your food. Pallet crafts will enable you to have the courage to invite some of your guests to have a chat with you as you make the food.

We are going to gather a few projects for you, so you can start somewhere. But before we check on that, it is important to see what the modern kitchen should have. Psychologically, there must be that fireplace that you use often to cook hard meals. You should not use wood because it can be risky over time. We understand that you can buy the best kitchen furniture but do they have the value of your money? The answer to this is upon you, but this is to be an eye opener to help you start considering wood pallet for your kitchen. We have already seen the advantages of pallets and it applies to all projects because pallets will remain to be pallets. We do have a trend where kitchens are known to have sophisticated appliances. But if you are the kind of person who has that personalized taste of everything, you can start learning how to turn wooden pallets to stunning furniture. We will share with you various ideas of pallet projects that will help you create a beautiful kitchen, in the most affordable manner.

Pallet Kitchen Cupboards

Having said that, the kitchen must have open space so that when you are busy with cooking a large amount of food, you are able to invite coworkers to the kitchen to help you cook. We have the cupboards that are essential in the kitchen. They are meant to store the kitchen tools and other accessories. They should be strong and secure; yes. we agree at some point that all the kitchen tools must be kept clean at all times. With pallet wood, you can come up with a complete mobile cupboard that can give the desired services. The boards that are usually used for the purpose are always very heavy but the pallet wood is very light and that is why you will find many people are going for pallet wood.

Kitchen Pallet Shelves

The permanent shelves are also very important when it comes to storing those items that are not always used. Pallet wood is very light and this makes it possible for them to be fixed on the wall with no difficulty. majority of people will go for the metal shelves because they believe that they are long-lasting; but remember, a kitchen is a place where water is plentiful and readily available.

This makes the place to have high moisture content. If the metal shelves are exposed to large amounts of moisture, the metal and the oxygen will react, forming rust, thereby destroying the metal. The wood pallet, on the other hand, has been treated in such a way that it can no longer absorb any water from the atmosphere and this makes the best material for kitchen wall shelve.

Another advantage about the pallet craft is that one can design whatever they want, either small or big. We have been brainwashed by the fact that the kitchen should not be well-equipped because it is only meant for the food. This is very wrong and you should make it look good because it is next to the dining room.

THE KITCHEN PALLET COOKING STOOL

Instead of going for the expensive wooden stools in store, you can buy pallets and make your own stools, which are friendly and cheap. Everyone wants to be known in the world of inventions; you can take ideas and put them into practice and come up with unique pallet craft products and this will give you extra income. We have had people who have started developing wood pallet sinks; they are skillfully made to make the kitchen work easier. The point of contact between the sink and the wood pallet are coated with aluminum, so that the water cannot destroy the wood. The sink pallet is very beautiful and good to work on. They reduce injuries since they cannot pierce your hands while cleaning them.

They are also good because they last longer and cannot be easily broken. Most of us do like leaning on the sink as they do their daily work in the kitchen. This may result in the material warping, and make your sink look ugly. The best thing about the wooden pallet, is that it cannot bend but when it is old it will break, but after giving you the best service after a long period of time.

Pallet Gas Cylinder Stands

The pallet gas stand is another thing that was recently brought into existence. This a stand that is to hold you gas cylinder in place, while you will not have to place it on the floor, like before. You can place it inside the pallet stand and when it is not in use, you can safely lock it away. We have never thought of this, yet it is very important in the kitchen. When you are not around and the kids are in the house alone, you can lock it and they will not have access to it. It is safety furniture for those kids who want to try out everything that mom and dad usually do when they are home.

We have kitchens that have this gadget just under the sink, but they are very expensive and are not easily carried away when doing general cleaning and this is the reason why the wood pallet gas cylinder holder was invented.

They can also provide the cylinder with protection from high temperatures, such that when heat from other sources is high, the cylinder is protected from exploding. They can also be used to hold the stoves so that they are firm when making food.

Pallet Utensil Hangers And Shelves

We have small items in the kitchen that do not fit in kitchen drawers; they are manufactured in a way that they should be hanged on the wall. Most families do not think of finding wood to place it on so that you can fix hangers on them. Pallet wood can be used to make this better. You do not have to make holes on the wall by driving nails, just find a good pallet timber and fix it with the number of nails required and place it on the wall, this will appear in order and professionally done. The kitchen will look modernized and elegant.

For convenience to beginners, who wish to start a pallet project, it is important to check out the best and unique furniture and start working on how they can improve them, either for commercial purposes or for their own private use. A kitchen is the place where it should be kept attractive. The lighting system in the kitchen can be improved by introducing replaceable bulb covers so that the wood is brightened. It can be a hard task to fix all the needs of the kitchen because of the financial implication that is associated with it, but if you were to do it by using pallet wood, you would save a lot for yourself and get valuable and unique products.

CHAPTER FOUR

PALLET DINING ROOM FURNITURE

The dining room is yet another place that demands a careful finish. It can be very expensive to furnish a dining room if it is to be done according to the required standards. For those who have financial challenges, they can now afford a smile because there are ready materials that they can use to come up with a modern dining room that appears expensive. Pallets can be used to make furniture meant for the dining rooms too! A dining room is one of the rooms that has the least furniture in an average family. It can have the least amount of furniture, depending on the number of people that are going to use it. At times, you will find that you may host a large number of people and will need additional furniture so that you can be able to accommodate them all.

Additional dining equipment can be hard to source, but if you try your hand in the pallet craft, you will succeed in hosting and making your visitor and family members comfortable. Pallet crafts can be applied to the assembly of any furniture. When we use the term assembly, it basically means that the joints of the furniture must not use normal nails. The wood is curved in a way that they are fixed together to form furniture, like tables and armchairs. Getting back to the dining room, you will appreciate the fact that there are several things that can be improved in the dining room with pallet wood. It is important to note some of the furniture that is found in an average dining room. You can choose to have the following, depending on your taste and personal demand.

Pallet Circular Dining Table

The dining table has been known to be either square or rectangular. The rectangular and circular tables are specific shapes that are always made for a particular class of people. They are meant to fit in irregular rooms that may not be squares or rectangular. Pallet wood can give you tables that have the ability to be positioned in any room. For those people who love the triangular tables, such that they accommodate three individuals, then this is the ideal shape for them. One major advantage of this kind of the table is that it will be easier to carry around and you can simply clean it because it is an assembly of pieces of stringers. Pallet wood is also very light, making the tables light. The dining room will look unique, blended by the unique shape of the tables in it. The square table is very common in every dining room but you can make it look good by using the pallet wood. Wooden pallets as we have already seen do come in various shapes.

One unique shape is the circular shape wooden pallet; they are used in the transportation of the electric cables and the plastic ropes in bulk. Once they have finished their job, most of the companies will discard them, or on rare occasions, they are sold to those companies that recycle wood for other purposes. The circular wooden pallet can be used to make circular dining table that can serve up to seven adults. How do you make a circular wooden pallet to be a table? You just need to carefully remove one top cover, then you put it upside down. The remaining cover will be used as the top for a table. Of course, you have to make it look professional by adding varnish so that it cannot clash with modern dining rooms.

The circular wooden pallet is a little bit complicated, such that it is very heavy because it is made up of many pieces of pallet wood for stability. This is the best for your dining table because it will appear firm and stable, and will not easily break. On the other hand, rectangular tables are easy to make because you only need to do a few calculations in terms of the amount of timber you will need. Pallet wooden tables can be made to suit the color of your walls, so the dining room can match with the furniture that is found there. When the dining room looks elegant, your appetite will just come by itself. This statement can look too original, but it is a fact.

Wooden Pallet Dining Chairs

The dining room will be incomplete without well-designed chairs. The chairs, too, can be given a good design when they are made of pallet wood. The common timber, that is normally used to make chairs, have a small width, making it difficult to use, considering the pressure from thin materials. The wooden pallet provides a good sitting allowance base with the required comfort. We all have experienced new wooden furniture and we can conclude that it has a certain common texture that is not friendly to your skin. Wooden pallets are very soft and are comfortable to use in the first place. You can order one if you do not have the expertise to construct. There are so many carpenters that are willing to take the job and do it the way you want, The pallet seat is flexible and can accommodate any size human being. They are very admirable and people will be asking you how you came up with the design. Pallet wood, that is meant for the construction of the dining chairs, doesn't need to be cut they are just grooved to the required shape.

Pallet Dining Room Shelves Cabinets And Drawers

Another idea in the dining room are the drawers that are sometimes not available. At some point you will need them for storing things like the toothpicks. You can design one with the pallet wood, such that people will access them without leaving the dining room to collect anything in the kitchen. We also have the dining pallet shelf for keeping the salt dishes. They are easily made and can be designed to suit your family needs. Let us consider someone challenged with heights; we can construct adjustable pallet shelves to make life simple in the dining room. The dining room, when not in use, can be converted to a study room. Some families have done this before, but to be precise, when the dining room is not in use, the chairs can be made to be multipurpose.

Children, at some point, can prove to be very destructive. They can scratch the dining room furniture, not with a bad intentions, but when they are playing. The pallet wood has been hardened and scratching it with a bare hand can be difficult. They are designed so that they can be smooth enough not to allow penetration of sharp objects. One good thing about the dining rooms all over is that they are always at a Conner that is well ventilated, and the lighting system in them are good enough to accommodate furniture that can be introduced in it. There are several dining room pallet designs that can be adopted for a colorful dining room.

If you need a dining room that has the best furniture ever, you can start learning how to design furniture by yourself by pallet crafting. There is nothing satisfying like consuming services that are excellent, when it came from your own making. Think about any design and you will see people raising questions on how to imitate what you have done. Pallet wood is the gold coating of the modern day furniture. Try the skills of pallet crafting and you will never regret it. Wooden pallet furniture takes a long time before it is replaced.

CHAPTER FIVE

OUTDOOR WOODEN PALLET FURNITURE

For cohesiveness, to be part of pallet crafts, sometimes it is important to give pallet furniture a comprehensive touch. A comfortable and firm couch can make relaxation at home feel like a garden. You can use recycled wooden pallets to come up with classic outdoor furniture; it is all about creativity and again, you have to believe that you can come up with your own self-made pallet crafts. Pallet crafting can give you the value of your money, such that the cheap pressboards that are sold in the stores will no longer be in your home. Outdoor furniture is one of the categories of furniture that suits wooden pallets. There is a number of furniture that can be constructed using the wooden pallet.

The outdoor furniture ranges from indoor benches to beer pint tables. Most of the people get confused in regards to finding out the amount of money they are going to spend for decent outdoor furniture, meant for relaxation. If you are part of this lot, then here is the good news; you can come up with different types of furniture with wooden pallets.

Pallets are readily available and cheap. You can take your time and do your own research; the furniture that is readily-made in stores that are made up of the wooden pallet are more expensive than those that are made up of normal timber. Instead of going to buy them, you can get the discarded wooden pallet and make your own unique furniture that can be used for a long period of time. You will also enjoy your own work; how does it feel when you see your friends enjoying the comfort of your own imagination? This can be great.

Outdoor furniture is meant for relaxation when you are tired and when you want to pass time with friends. Remember the outdoor furniture are always outside and they are prone to low temperatures and the bleaching factor; we can also have the sun rays that is very bad when it comes to furniture. Thanks to the wooden pallet that is resistant to adverse climatic conditions, they cannot change easily their color and also they can last for a long time outside without developing cracks. Let us look at the outdoor furniture that can be used for the purpose.

Wooden Pallet Outdoor Benches

Benches can sound very simple to make but the most important thing about them is that they have to be given a unique finish so that it does not only become comfortable but also beautiful. You can choose from many varieties that are all over right from the neighbors. Just by the use of a wooden pallets, you can get a personalized bench that is eye-catching and comfortable. Artwork does not need to please every person that comes across it but it should satisfy the artist that at least have made something that can be utilized for a purpose. Benches made from the pallet wood are of the best size and can be carried around within the compound; this means they can be made to be mobile.

We have those people who love basking in the sun rays; it is just a matter of thinking where to source the wooden pallet, and then carrying out a research on the numerous designs that are available. If you find that you are not pleased with any craft pallets designs that are available, then we are all free to come up with designs that are personally pleasing.

PERSONALIZED OUTDOOR COUCHES

Wooden pallets are products that can be used to make any furniture; they have been around for a long time. There are very many ideas that are available for the wooden pallets. For outdoor couches, every person has their own taste.

People are of different character and don't live in the same setup. Wooden pallets are the same all over; this makes the materials to be flexible and any person can develop their own design for the desired furniture. During that year-end party, when you have invited your colleagues for a barbecue, the couches can offer them extraordinary comfort, yet you constructed them with very cheap and readily available wooden pallets. People are obsessed with prices; wooden pallets are cheap but they produce long-lasting products of high quality, compared to the hurriedly assembled furniture.

For you to make this outdoor furniture, you have to believe in your potential to come up with new ideas, just by looking at what someone else did and developing yours; as simple as that. Wooden pallets outdoor furniture are great since they do not lose their heat so easily and they can keep you warm during that cold weather, especially when you have to use them early in the morning or very late in the evening.

OUTDOOR CHAIRS

Chairs are not only meant for indoor purposes; this traditional belief was correct when people had not realized that there are other materials that can be used to construct chairs that can be placed outside. They relied on metal or plastic chairs that were very expensive. Wooden pallets chairs are very comfortable, more especially when they are designed to have an arm holder and some stringers that can provide the space to step on.

This will provide an added luxury because your legs cannot remain hanging in the air. You don't need to have a lot of money so that you have high-quality comfort. They are easily moved from one region to another, right from the balcony of the house and even outside. Pallet chairs can be designed to give the person the healthiest posture.

We are human beings with complicated structures; pallets are materials that can be used to invent furniture that that best fits in the posture that makes you comfortable when you sit on it. Wooden pallet chairs will make you feel like you should not be told to leave that chair.

OUTDOOR WOODEN PALLET TABLES

Wooden pallet tables are of many different kinds; they can permanently fixate on the ground or they can be designed to be able to move from place to place. The disadvantage about the permanent outdoor table is that you may want to move the table within the compound. You have come across this situation where you are hanging out with your friends and suddenly the table comes down with all the beer pints; this will not happen to the wooden pallet tables. They are firm and strong. Hanging out with colleagues or an outdoor meeting, you will have the participants have that original look of the furniture within.

A stress-free environment is contributed by its uniqueness; the furniture around every place will add value to your relaxation and also elevate your class. Furniture made from wooden pallets do not go with fashion; they are always trending because of its originality. You can create an original from very few wood pallets.

They are functional for both outdoor and indoor activities. Wooden pallets are very easy to work with. They just need wax to add a little glitter on it, or a few varnishes on top, and the table is ready for any outdoor activity or an indoor occasion. This tables look professionally made and you can also make 1 this, if you have the determination to make one. Believe in your potential to do something great with the wooden pallet.

CHAPTER SIX

EASY TO MAKE ACCESSORIES

Pallet wood is very easy to assemble so that they can make, not only furniture, but also some small accessories that can make you live a happy, comfortable life. In life, you don't have to tag everything to expensive accessories so that life becomes sweet. You have to look around and make use of the locally available materials, and everything else will follow.

Do you want an eye-catching focal point with a relaxed seating? I know this a simple yes. Wooden pallet furniture can be a good source of mental relaxation in the outdoors. They are cheap and easy to make. Garden accessories from used pallet wood are also another idea to add life to your compound. There are thousands of garden designs that can be made using the wooden pallet.

The art of inventing something to satisfy a certain need does not need any technical knowledge at all; it only requires a stable mind and the ability to create new things from recyclable materials, like the used pallet wood.

Wooden pallet recycling is very eco-friendly and economical, in terms of space and finances. They can be assembled quickly and they will provide a practical solution to outdoor and indoor decoration.

One more thing that you must know is that wooden pallet furniture needs care, no matter how they are treated, they need to be painted and waxed. By doing this, you will make the furniture dirt free.

Check out these ideas, to begin with, and you will find yourself in a position to come up with your own ideas that can suit best to your needs. Recyclable wooden pallets can be used to assemble the following accessories.

Wooden Pallet Wine Racks And Glass Racks

Almost every restaurant and dining room have this equipment; they are very important in the care of the most expensive glasses. This can be made from wooden pallets and give that house the beauty that it deserves. The pallet can be cut into the required size and fit in the rooms. For the glass to remain tidy, you will need to have the wooden pallet rack. They will not only remain clean but they will remain protected from breakages, since the pallet rack can be fixed on the wall so that nothing cause it to fall. The racks will bring you the country memories by making the room look original and give a taste of unique tradition. The wine, especially the old brands, will fit in well and take it back to its original taste.

PALLET FLOWER BEDS

This is another idea that has been very effective with pallet wood. The pallet flower beds are functional to those homes that are highly raised; we have some green decors that require light that has been abstracted by the building. Wooden pallets can be used to give the flowers an elevation that is needed. You can use wooden pallets to create beautiful sceneries in your compound and are designed so they can be fixed on the wall, particularly for the climbing and the crawling herbs. Not only the flowers, we have some beautiful fruits that are doing well when caged in this way. Wooden pallets will add beauty to your home, without necessarily going for the expensive flower vases that cannot be enough for the job.

OTHER SIMPLE FIXABLE ACCESSORIES

PALLET LAMP HOLDERS

This is another accessory that will add elegance to your bedroom or study room. People have been going for this gadget in stores for a long time. Pallet wood can be used to make one that will look modern. They are sold expensively, but you can make yours and make the table look uniquely designed. The pallet lamp stand can also be fixed on the table permanently to give it stability and firmness. This idea is simple to design.

THANKSGIVING GIFTS PALLET CRAFTING IDEAS

Do you want to appreciate that family member who has done something great for you? If you are in the position of giving out gifts when you visit someone, there are so many pallet crafting ideas that can make up the gifts for a visitation. Gifts are meant to bring memories and to remind people how much you care about them. You don't have to think of very expensive gifts. Go for the materials that are cheap and easily assembled. The pallet gifts are very cheap yet can mean a lot to the recipient. In this case, you have to add some paint so that the gift looks beautiful, especially if it is to be given to a kid or someone that means a lot to you. Wooden pallets are the best materials for gifts because they are quickly assembled to a structure that can appear expensive, but are actually cheap. Most importantly, the message will be passed to the recipients in a unique manner.

Gifts can be expensive but they have to be unique so that the people receiving them will be able to reconnect with the motive intended to be conveyed.

Pallet Envelope Holders

If you are the kind of person who thinks before spending, this is an accessory that you are not supposed to miss in any way; it is very easy to create. Once developed, it can be fixed in a place where everyone can gain access easily. Wooden pallet envelope holders are easily fixable on the wall and can be painted to match the wall color, making the house will appear unique and extraordinary. This craft idea is cheap to construct; it can take you a few hours to fix one.

We are talking about two hours to be certain. You only need two pieces of the wood pallet to make one envelope holder. This idea can be designed to any shape that is convenient to you. They are available in stores but they are not worth buying because you can make one at home and it will serve the same duty. If you are looking to have one for your home, then you only need to find a few pieces of wooden pallet stringers and practically you can make one.

Wooden Pallet Hangers

There are some accessories that a normal human being should not go buying them from the shop. Like this cloth hanger, that is very simple to make. They are easily compatible with the grooving technique. We all admire that bedroom that has a colorful look, where sleep comes automatically. This is the simplest pallet craft that we sometimes see children try to make.

They can be made in such a way that they can fit in the bedroom, without noticing that they are made up discarded pieces of pallet wood. Finally, the pallet hangers are very light and can also be coated with a golden brown paint to add a little bit of brightness. The worry is, the paint can peel off but the way to avoid the inconvenience is very simple; you don't have to use it immediately because pallet wood takes some time to absorb paint the dry up. Allow it to dry well before taking it to the wardrobe to hang clothes on. Pallet crafting does not rule out any idea; you can develop any and come up with a unique product for your own personal use or for commercial purposes.

In conclusion, every human being has the potential to create anything out of nothing. We have different skills that do not need someone to remind us to explore them and bring them to reality. Pallet crafting is one of the arts that every other person can begin and succeed within a very short time. Wooden pallets have made it possible for the world to enjoy products that are manufactured globally.

They are very important equipment in business and are discarded on a daily basis. It is important to educate the public on the general importance of recycling wooden pallets so that trees can be preserved for the coming generation. If we were to use them for everything that we do, the trees will cease to exist. It is important for every individual to start embracing the fact that wooden pallets can be used, even after being used in the transport industry. Creativity is inborn; we are all installed with a unique ability to create something that can improve our lives. The wooden pallet can give the best home accessories, creatively designed.

Thank you!

Lightning Source UK Ltd.
Milton Keynes UK
UKOW05f1944090517
300856UK00011B/569/P

9 781541 051195